great gardens
for kids

great gardens
for kids

Clare Matthews

Photographs by Clive Nichols

hamlyn

First published in Great Britain in 2002 by Hamlyn
a division of Octopus Publishing Group Limited,
2–4 Heron Quays, London E14 4JP

Copyright © Octopus Publishing Group Limited 2002
Photographs © Clive Nichols

Distributed in the United States and Canada by
Sterling Publishing Co., Inc.
387 Park Avenue South, New York, NY 10016-8810

A CIP record for this book is available from the
British Library.

ISBN 0 600 60516 7

The author and publishers have made every effort to
ensure that all instructions and ideas given in this book
are accurate and safe, but they cannot accept liability for
any resulting injury, damage or loss to either person or
property whether direct or consequential and howsoever
arising. The author and publishers will be grateful for any
information that will assist them in keeping future
editions up to date.

Measurements Both imperial and metric measurements
have been given throughout this book. When following
instructions, you should choose to work in either metric
or imperial, and never mix the two.

Printed and bound in China

contents

introduction

With a little imagination and ingenuity, any garden, however small, can become a fascinating and stimulating place for children to play. More often, however, children's needs are poorly served in the garden – an afterthought resulting in some small concession or, more frequently, in a random assemblage of unattractive play equipment parents wish they could do without.

This book brings a creative, fresh approach to children's needs, and shows how to make unusual, captivating and attractive features which can be integrated into a family garden, or which can be carefully woven together to produce separate spaces dedicated to games, fun and fantasy.

Projects and inspirational case studies reveal practical and affordable ways any garden can be transformed into a children's paradise; a landscape that inspires imaginative play, provides physical challenges, appeals to the senses and nurtures an interest in nature and horticulture. In short, a safe place where children can explore, learn and relax on their own terms.

Clockwise from top left *Climbing Wall (see page 20), Wildlife Container Pond (see page 78), Rill (see page 50), Foldaway Playhouse (see page 28).*

The emphasis is on providing play features that children will really love – they are chosen with both children's needs and style in mind. Throughout the book, colour and decoration make a strong contribution to the projects and gardens, which are designed to appeal to children but are not childish. Whether the garden is traditional or contemporary, flamboyantly colourful or rustic, there are projects that can be tailored to suit each style and become a harmonious part of the overall design.

Creating a children's garden not only provides hours of happy fulfilling play, but addressing children's needs makes them feel valued and gives them a great pride in their garden. The more that children are allowed to contribute their ideas and take part in the physical business of a garden's creation, the greater that pride will be. All of the projects described here are straightforward and require no special skills, just enthusiasm and creativity on the part of both parents and children.

Above right and right *Plant a garden with all five senses in mind, to allow children to experiment with what they find around them. Touch is especially rewarding; choose plants with a variety of textures – smooth, soft, crinkly, rough, velvety or fleshy.*

Opposite page clockwise from top left *Pet Palace (see page 74), Strawberry Tower (see page 66), Daffodil Maze (see page 22), Sailing Boat Sandpit (see page 12).*

active play

Climbing, swinging, jumping, running and simply letting off steam are important parts of outdoor play. Using an imaginative approach, it is possible to create unusual and appealing equipment that provides the opportunity for children to test and develop their physical confidence while they play. A well thought-out array of equipment allows children to acquire skills and a confidence in their abilities, which can be learned in no other way. It is important that physical challenges are demanding, so the child experiences a real feeling of triumph and achievement. However, it is also important that steps are taken to make activities and equipment as safe as possible. However robust, equipment will suffer from wear and tear and should be checked regularly for signs of damage and fatigue. When planning an area for physical games, consider both the age and size of the children who will use it – if possible add elements which can be changed to provide new challenges, such as the Climbing Wall (see page 20). All the projects in this chapter are designed to look appealing and provide hours of really exciting physical play.

Sailing Boat Sandpit • Rope Spider's Web • Pebble Mosaic Hopscotch • Climbing Wall • Daffodil Maze

sailing boat sandpit

It is with good reason that a sandpit is considered an essential part of gardens for young children. Even the most modest sandpit can provide hours of amusement. Sand provides the opportunity for creative and constructive play, and is ideal for fine-tuning the motor skills of young children. What is more, it is a valuable prop in fantasy games, where even humble sand pies can become cream buns. Just provide assorted scoops, spoons, cups and buckets. Decorated as a sailing boat, this stylish sandpit has an added appeal to inspire imaginative play.

materials

large tyre
mid blue multisurface
   spray paint
bath sponge
bright blue acrylic paint
13mm (^{1}/$_2$in) diameter
   wooden dowel
tack
turquoise and blue kite fabric
weed-suppressing membrane
play sand

Choosing materials

Choose a clean tyre without any obvious damage. The kite fabric can be any colour you like; the beauty of it is that it doesn't need to be hemmed – simply cut it to size.

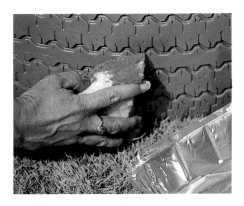

1 Thoroughly clean the largest tyre available and allow to dry. Paint it using a multisurface spray paint. Cut a bath sponge into a wave shape and, using acrylic paint, sponge waves around the tyre in a contrasting blue.

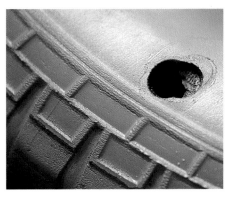

2 Make a hole for the mast in the wall of the tyre, using a 13mm (¹/₂in) wood drill bit. Push in the length of dowel and secure it in an upright position with a tack through the base of the tyre into the bottom of the dowel.

3 Cut a triangular sail from kite fabric to fit the mast, allowing extra width for a turning along its vertical side wide enough for the dowel to slip through. Sew the turning over and slip the sail over the mast. Top it with a blue flag made in the same way.

4 Line the base of the sandpit with weed-suppressing membrane or thick polythene sheeting and fill it with sand. It may be necessary to cover the sandpit when not in use to prevent animals from soiling the sand.

rope spider's web

This robust rope climbing challenge is enormous fun. Made from seemingly natural materials, this vast web is cunningly composed of a combination of simple knots, making its construction within the reach of anyone who can tie a knot in the corner of their hankie! Not only is the web superb for climbing and swinging, its unusual form makes it a splendid prop for fantasy games. The web can be adapted to fit any space, and also presents an attractive solution to separating or screening off parts of the garden. Though the rope used here appears natural, it is a craftily disguised synthetic rope. It is important to use a strong synthetic rope, as it will resist rot far more efficiently than natural fibres, which may perish in just a few seasons. As with all play equipment, however, it is important to check regularly for signs of deterioration.

materials

2 large wooden posts,
   4m (12ft) long
ready-mix concrete
30m (100ft) of 3-strand
   hempex rope
sticky tape

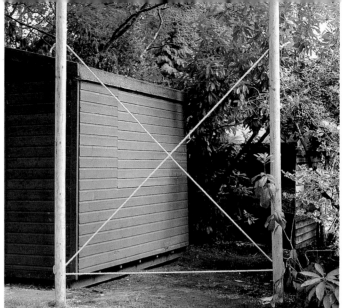

1 Dig two holes 1m (3ft) deep and 2m (6ft) apart, stand the posts in the holes and pack ready-mix concrete around them. Ensure that they are vertical. When the concrete has set, drill two holes 10cm (4in) apart near the top of each post and another pair about 30cm (12in) from the ground. Add another single hole at the centre point on both posts, making sure all the holes are at corresponding heights on the two posts.

2 Thread a length of rope through the lower of the top pair of holes on the first post. Pass it diagonally to the higher of the bottom holes on the second post. Take it back through the lowest hole on the same post to the lowest hole on the first post. Then back through the adjacent hole on that post and diagonally to the lower hole at the top of the second post. Pull the rope tight and secure it with overhand knots (see page 16).

3 Tie a length of rope between the two uppermost holes and another between the central holes. Again use an overhand knot to secure them on each side. Keep all ropes as taut as possible. Add a length of rope vertically across the centre of the web.

4 Attach it to the centre point of the uppermost horizontal rope using a cargo knot (see page 16), finished off with an overhand knot. Pass it across the centre, tying an overhand knot around the criss-crossing ropes and finish off with a cargo knot followed by an overhand knot at the centre of the lowest horizontal rope.

5 Starting from the centre, spiral the remaining rope round the framework. Start with a cargo knot finished with an overhand knot at the centre and tie a cargo knot each time the rope crosses another. Take care to keep the ropes taut, but do not distort the web. Finish off using a cargo knot followed by an overhand knot and the web is complete.

How to tie an overhand knot

An overhand knot is the simplest of knots. Simply loop one end behind the other, pass it through and pull tight.

How to tie a cargo knot

1 Cargo knots require passing one rope end through another. This process is made easier by binding the rope end with tape.

2 Start by passing the bound end of the rope up between the strands where you want the knot to be.

3 Take the end back round in front of itself, up behind the horizontal arm, back through the loop to the front.

4 Pull the rope taut and continue with the loose end. Use this knot to join one rope to another as you pass it.

Right *Here a crossbeam and ladder have been added to the sturdy structure for extra climbing fun.*

pebble mosaic hopscotch

Going from here to there is much more fun if it is done with a hop and a jump. This traditional game has been reproduced in attractive pebble mosaic paving stones. They can be set into a gravel or grassy path, arranged in a patio, or form stepping stones across a well-trodden patch of lawn. The mosaics are incredibly durable and deceptively straightforward to make. The same technique could be used to produce purely decorative stones with patterns, or perhaps initials or words.

materials
4 offcuts of timber, 2.5cm (1in)
    square and 30cm (12in) long
nails
black pebbles
white pebbles
polythene sheet
cement

1 Make a simple mould by nailing the four pieces of wood together into a basic square shape. Make the square the size you want the finished mosaic paving slabs to be.

Decorating the slabs

Slabs with numbers can be laid out to form a hopscotch board. However, many different designs can be used – try initials, letters or simple patterns.

2 Using black and white pebbles, lay out the first number in the frame. Start with the border and the number in dark pebbles, then fill in the background in white pebbles. Any simple design will work. Carefully remove the frame to leave the pebbles in place.

3 Place the frame on a polythene sheet and almost fill it with cement. Transfer the pebbles from the design to the cement, pushing them well in. Leave overnight before removing the frame. The cement takes one week to reach full strength.

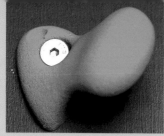

climbing wall

Perhaps the ultimate climbing challenge you can provide, this colourful climbing wall is straightforward to construct. It is made from two sheets of plyboard which are attached to vertical posts in the ground, and have climbing holds fixed to them. The aim is to progress along the wall without touching the ground, rather than climbing to alarming heights. Climbing only a small distance from the ground, however, does not diminish the task nor the sense of achievement as the child stretches arms and legs, clinging with fingers and toes to the holds. The climbing challenge can easily be changed and made more demanding by simply rearranging the holds. This wall is designed for pre-school children, but could easily be scaled up to suit older children.

materials
2 sheets of 18mm ($^3/_4$in) marine
  plyboard
PVA primer
wood-preserving stain
climbing holds with T-nuts
5cm (2in) countersunk bolts
3 wooden posts, 7.5cm (3in)
  square and 2m (6ft) long
9 large bolts
ready-mix concrete

1 Coat the sheets of plyboard with a solution of one part PVA to one part water. Mark the positions of the holds and drill holes using a 10mm ($^3/_8$in) wood drill bit at each location. Drill more holes than you have holds, so that the challenge can be changed later on. The distance between the holds should be challenging but not disconcerting.

2 Paint the boards with wood-preserving stain. Choose a colour to suit its location. This climbing wall is bright and cheerful, but choosing greens or browns would render it less obtrusive in the garden.

3 Securely push a T-nut into each hole in the board from the back. Attach the climbing holds to the front of the boards using the countersunk bolts to fix them in place. Take the time to devise a demanding climbing route across the wall, but also an appealing arrangement of holds in different shapes and different colours.

4 Bolt the boards on to the fronts of the three square posts, so that they form a continuous board. Use three bolts for each post. Dig three holes, 75cm (30in) deep, set the posts in position and pack ready-mix concrete around them in the holes. Ensure that the wall is held vertical until the concrete sets hard. The 'rock face' is now ready for climbers.

daffodil maze

More correctly, this sparkling display of the fragrant narcissus 'Yellow Cheerfulness' is a labyrinth of blooms. Two interlocked spirals of flower form a path from one side of the maze to the other, firstly spiralling into the centre and then spiralling out again in the opposite direction. This vast display is not only fascinating and attractive, it makes a wonderful place to play. Walking slowly through the maze, concentrating on every step is totally absorbing, but add some friends and the maze lends an extra challenge to lively chasing games. You can never be quite sure if your pursuer is on the same path as you. From the moment that the first shoots emerge, delineating the pattern of paths, the maze is a magnet to children. The flowers last six weeks in good conditions. Work starts on the maze in the autumn.

materials
2 long ropes
daffodil bulbs (about 150 per
  metre/yard of maze)
grit (optional)

1 Using two ropes, lay out the design. Ropes can be easily adjusted to get the perfect shape. If possible, check the design from above.

2 Laying out the bulbs around the maze will ensure you have sufficient for the proposed design. This maze has a diameter of 8m (24ft).

3 Arrange the bulbs in a single layer on the grass, closely following the lines of the ropes. Reduce the width of the lines of bulbs as they come towards the centre of the maze.

4 Lift out sections of turf to create planting areas about twice the depth of the bulbs. Arrange the bulbs randomly in the hole and replace the turf. Continue around the maze. If the soil is heavy and moisture retentive, add a layer of grit to the base of the hole before putting in the bulbs.

Using a bulb planter

For smaller designs, a long-handled bulb planter could be used. Simply remove a plug of turf with the planter, pop the bulb into the hole, pointed end upwards, then replace the turf and tread down lightly.

Below *As the bulbs emerge, the maze soon takes shape. As soon as the growth is obvious enough not to be trampled, play can begin in the maze.*

Left and right *The sheer exuberance of the* Narcissus *'Yellow Cheerfulness' makes it an excellent choice, plus it is a robust late flowerer which naturalizes well. This maze does require a lavish use of bulbs but they should return year after year, making the maze a seasonal treat, a celebration of the return of warmer weather. For a smaller space, the whole concept could be simplified – even a wiggling pathway of bright flowers and foliage could provide hours of entertainment.*

Left *After flowering, the maze must be left for six weeks before mowing, to allow the bulbs to build up energy for next year's flush of flowers, so a hidden corner may be the best location for the maze.*

a place
of their own

Whatever form it takes, children of all ages revel in the privacy and opportunity a place of their own affords. A playhouse, den or hideaway is an important part of any children's garden. For younger children, it is a secure intimate space where they can feel comfortable to initiate all kinds of fantasy play. Whatever the playhouse's actual shape, size or theme, in the powerfully imaginative mind of a young child it can become anything from a spaceship to a zoo, a stage for role-playing games. As children grow older, a den forms an important function as a private place to share with friends. A place to read, invent games and relax on their own terms.

In providing a playhouse or hideaway, there are a number of points to consider. First, its location; if chosen carefully, even a children's den can make a positive contribution to the appearance of the garden. Select a hideaway which is in sympathy with the style of the garden and plan its position carefully. What might look at home in a rural situation is unlikely to look appealing in an urban courtyard. Second, consider the ages of the children who are going to use it – a toddler paradise is unlikely to appeal to a seven-year-old.

Foldaway Playhouse • Flowery Hideaway • Suspended Tent • Vine Tepee

foldaway playhouse

Where space is limited, a playhouse which can be folded away is a splendid solution. Anchored to any solid vertical structure, this cheerful little hideaway takes only seconds to fold or unfold, bringing variety to the garden. The absence of a roof is irrelevant to younger children who will feel at ease in the intimate space the playhouse creates. There is plenty of room for two or three toddlers and their toys. Changing the painted decoration will change the appeal of the house. Painted brown it becomes a log cabin, paint it grey and add crenellations and it becomes a castle – the possibilities are endless. The playhouse is reasonably durable, but may need protecting from the worst of the winter weather.

materials

4 pieces of 8mm (^{1}/$_4$in) exterior-
   grade plyboard, 50x110cm
   (20x44in)
1 piece of 8mm (^{1}/$_4$in) exterior-grade
   plyboard, 120x110cm (48x44in)
   and rising to a point
PVA primer
acrylic paints
5cm (2in) wide Velcro fastenings
strong glue
staple gun
8 small blocks of timber
tacks
5 metal hooks and eyes

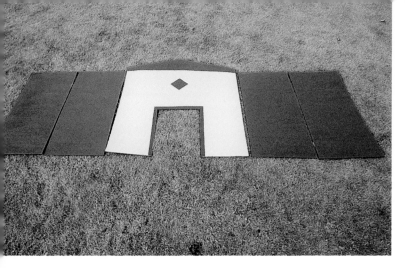

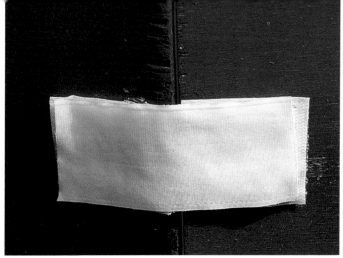

1 Cut the pieces of plyboard to size and seal the panels with a solution of one part PVA and one part water and leave to dry. Paint them with acrylic paint and leave to dry again. Lay the pieces flat on the ground face down, as if the house has been opened out.

2 Use strong glue and a staple gun to attach two sets of Velcro squares on one side of each panel so that it can be joined to the next. Fix the longer strips of Velcro to the opposite sides so the panels can be joined together to form the house.

3 Prop the house into position and tack a block of wood to each of the inside front corners at the top. Fix a metal eye on one block and the corresponding hook on the adjacent block on both corners of the house. Tack two more blocks on to the edges of the house where it meets the wall, and the remaining blocks on to the wall itself. Screw the eyes into the blocks on the house and the hooks on the wall to hold the structure rigid and secure.

4 To fold the house away, loosen the Velcro straps and unfasten the front safety hooks. Push the centres of the two sides towards each other to collapse the house. Use another hook on the reverse of the front panel to secure it to the wall.

flowery hideaway

The tiniest of hideaways are attractive to children. This flowering bower takes up little space and is appealing enough to take pride of place on the patio or even balcony; although it would look equally at ease set in an herbaceous border. The unexpected presence of a secluded space amid the flowers makes this secret hideaway especially appealing. The twining stems of clematis rapidly cover the framework; within just a few weeks there is a feeling of privacy. Carefully choosing the clematis ensures the bower is decked with colourful flowers throughout the summer, while a fragrant skirt of petunias clothes the sides of the pots.

materials

5 large pots
blue masonry paint
aluminium foil
newspaper
crocks
compost
5 clematis plants
petunia plants
5 iron poles
silver metal paint
galvanized wire

1 Choose five large containers. Here, inexpensive terracotta has been livened up with soft blue masonry paint. When the paint has dried, line the pots with aluminium foil.

2 Next line the pots with a good layer of newspaper, to help retain moisture and keep roots cool. Add a layer of crocks to the bases of the containers.

3 Fill with compost and plant the clematis 5cm (2in) deeper than in their original pots. This gives the plants a chance to regrow, should clematis wilt strike.

4 Next plant petunias around the edges of the pots. Place the five pots in a circle and, using five iron poles painted silver, create the frame of the tepee. Finish with a spiral of silver wire wound around the frame, leaving an opening to form the door.

Choosing plants

Choose a selection of plants to fit in with the colour scheme in your garden. These are **Clematis** *'Comtesse de Bouchaud' and 'Multi Blue', with* **Petunia** *'Pastel'.*

suspended tent

When suspended from any convenient tree or shrub, this brightly coloured tent makes a spacious den. The tent is crafted from kite fabric, which is durable, light and easy to work with, as it does not fray when cut. Simple sand bags weight the corners as a safer alternative to tent pegs, which could of course be used instead. Bright and cheerful, the tent provides an ideal temporary summer residence. Packed into a small bag, it is fun to take on holiday or even picnics.

materials
blue kite fabric
purple kite fabric
cotton
metal eyelets and
    fixing tool
sand
cleats

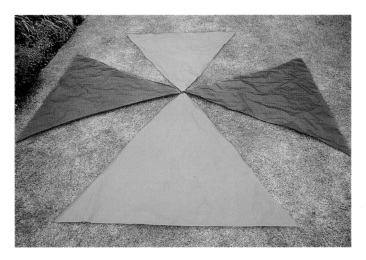

1 Cut four identical triangles of kite fabric, each with a base of 160cm (64in) and a height of 170cm (68in). Sew them together using simple running stitch, so that the colours alternate.

2 Fit a metal eyelet into each corner of the tent and another one through its apex. These simple eyelets are attached using a hammer and a special fixing tool.

3 Use more kite fabric to create four sand bags, approximately 20x30cm (8x12in). Turn them right sides out, fill with sand, sew up the open edge and add a metal eyelet. Attach the bags to the corners of the tent using cleats.

4 Cut a 50cm (20in) vertical slit in the centre of one of the sides of the tent to create a door. Attach a cleat to the metal eye at the apex of the tent and use it to suspend the tent from a sturdy tree or shrub.

The fixings

Galvanized cleats and eyelets are easy to find in hardware or sailing shops. The eyelets come with a special fixing tool which is simple to use. Make sure the cleats fit through the eyelets.

vine tepee

Swathed in a rustling cloak of enormous, beautifully textured leaves, this simplest of structures provides a snug hideaway. It fits well in a green or wooded garden, or it could even be tucked discreetly in among established shrubs. In the autumn, the tepee becomes a glowing display of some of the season's most spectacular colours. Here a vitis, a vigorous tendril climber suited to partial shade, has been chosen but you could experiment with other leafy climbers to suit the proposed location.

materials
about 18 sturdy hazel poles,
   3m (10ft) long
hemp twine
5 *Vitis cognetiae* plants

1 The tepee is formed with stout hazel poles; the floor area is about 2m (6ft) in diameter. Start by pushing five of the poles firmly into the ground to make a circle, allowing them to cross at the centre of the circular area. Tie the tops with twine to secure.

2 Add more hazel poles equally spaced around the tepee, not forgetting to leave a gap in the front of the circle to form the door. Tie all the rods securely together at the apex of the tepee using thick hemp twine, or other twine of a natural colour.

3 Cut three shorter lengths of hazel pole and tie them across the door space to leave just a small entrance at the bottom. Arrange five vines around the tepee, spacing them evenly.

4 Plant the vines close to the poles, angled towards the structure. Five plants give good coverage quickly, but fewer would do the job given time. Carefully encourage the vines on to the structure and keep well watered.

furniture

A table and chairs play a fundamental role in children's gardens, just as they do in one designed for adults. They are a focus for activities: they provide a place to eat, draw, paint, play and entertain friends. When choosing or creating garden furniture for children, it is important to consider the size of the children who will use it. Adult furniture is inappropriate for small children who have to make perilous climbs on to chairs and, once there, sit uncomfortably as they stretch to reach up to the table. Similarly, outgrown furniture would be uncomfortable for older children. Robust durability and safety are fundamental qualities to seek in children's garden furniture. Not only will it need to withstand the battering of the elements, it will also need to stand up to all kinds of rough treatment. Remember to make provision not just for your own children, but also your children's guests.

A place to eat or sit is best positioned slightly away from equipment designed for active play; the juxtaposition of two very different types of activities could easily cause conflict or even present a safety hazard. As always, ensure that the furniture chosen complements its surroundings. Decorative furniture can bring a vibrant splash of colour to the garden, while natural materials are less obtrusive. When thoughtfully placed, appealing furniture can also fulfil an additional ornamental role, providing an attractive focal point and drawing children into that area of the garden. The projects in this chapter produce simple, appealing furniture which children will really enjoy using.

'My Place' Mosaic Table • Grass Stools • Growing Bench

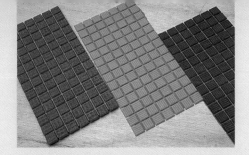

'my place' mosaic table

A table and chairs are a fundamental part of any children's garden. Here, a garden table past its best is given a new lease of life using richly coloured opaque glass mosaics and florist's beads. A randomly patterned background provides a foil for circular 'place mats' designed and completed by the children themselves, allowing each child their own individual creative input on a manageable scale as part of a larger family project. Mosaic is a wonderfully durable surface, with a timeless appeal. Any sturdy table could be used, so long as its size is appropriate to the children who will use it. Larger pieces of furniture could even be cut down if the integrity of their structure is preserved. If a wooden table is used, a coat of matching wood stain completes the transformation.

materials
2.5cm (1in) exterior-grade
    plyboard
PVA primer
screws
exterior tile adhesive
mosaic tiles
glass florist's beads
exterior tile grout

1 Cut the piece of plyboard to the exact size of the table top. Seal it with a solution of one part PVA to one part water. Allow to dry and screw it to the top of the table. Mark on the positions of the 'place mats' by drawing around a dinner plate. Mark guidelines along the centre of the board in both directions to give a centre point.

2 Apply the border tiles and those delineating the place mats by 'buttering' the back of each tile with tile adhesive and pushing it firmly into place, leaving a uniform gap between tiles.

3 Starting from the centre line and working out, randomly apply the background tiles. Cover large areas quickly by cutting the paper backing sheets of the mosaic tiles into blocks and pushing them evenly into a bed of tile adhesive applied to the table. Make the pattern random by cutting a few holes in the sheets and infilling with tiles of a different colour.

4 It will be necessary to clip tiles to fit around the 'place mats'. Use tile nippers. Score a line on the tile and break it using the nippers. (Wear gloves and safety goggles; this is not a task for children.) Leave to dry for at least four hours before removing the paper backing from the tiles, by dampening it and peeling it away.

5 Allow each child to work out the design for their 'place mat' on a piece of paper. Transfer the design into place on the table using either the 'buttering' method or pushing the pieces into a bed of adhesive.

6 When it is dry, spread grouting over the surface of the table, working it into the gaps between the tiles. Wipe off any excess with a damp cloth. Once dry, remove any final traces of grout on the tiles using a scourer.

grass stools

Placed around the garden, these grassy pots make wonderfully novel, child-sized stools. Here the pots have been painted a sunny yellow, but choose a colour to suit their location or let each child design and decorate their own stool. Camomile or creeping thyme would make interesting alternatives to turf, with the added appeal of a burst of fragrance each time they are used. Both plants would enjoy a sunny spot and can be trimmed to keep them neat and encourage a dense coverage. The stools, when weighted properly, are very stable but they are not suitable for young children to climb on.

materials
squat terracotta pots
masonry or acrylic paint
turfs
bricks
compost

1 Paint the pots using masonry or acrylic paints and allow to dry. Choose a colour to fit in with the rest of the garden.

2 When the paint is dry, invert the painted pot on a turf and cut around it with a sharp knife to cut out a circular piece of turf.

3 Pack the bottom of the pot with bricks to give it stability. Four bricks for each pot should be sufficiently heavy.

4 Fill the pots with compost to about 5cm (2in) from the tops of the pots. Firm down the compost well and smooth the surface.

5 Place the turf circle on top of the compost and gently firm it down. Water it well. A slightly domed finish is more attractive than a flat one. Keep the turf well watered and trimmed.

growing bench

This sturdy bench is formed from thick slabs of natural wood. The towering back forms a trellis, which can support climbing plants to form a living screen. Set the bench 60–90cm (24–36in) away from a fence or hedge and it forms a leafy 'rat run' behind it, ideal for chasing games or hide and seek. It can also be used to divide one area of the garden from another. Many climbing plants will clothe the trellis. For the best effect, pick a plant which will thrive in your chosen location. Clematis will make a pretty, flowery screen, while humulus will produce a covering of lush lime-green leaves each year. For a more shady location, x fatshedera, as used here, will give a tropical feel to the garden.

materials
large slab of wood
2 logs
2m (6ft) garden canes
hemp twine
climbing plants, such as
  x *Fatshedera lizei*

1 Choose a large slab of wood to make the seat of the bench. Use two equal sized logs to support it. It is important to make the bench the correct height for the children who are going to use it.

2 Use a 13mm ($^{1}/_{2}$in) wood drill bit to drill a series of holes along the back of the seat. Space the holes 10cm (4in) apart.

3 Set the two log supports into position. Place the seat on the supports, ensuring it is level. Push a cane through each hole in the back of the seat of the bench and push it firmly into the ground beneath. This gives the bench stability. For even greater rigidity, the seat can be screwed to the top of the logs.

4 Tie three canes horizontally across the vertical canes, using hemp twine to secure. Ensure that there are no dangerous ends protruding which could cause injury. Prepare the soil behind the bench and plant your chosen climbers. Encourage their progress up the canes and keep well watered until they are established.

water

Children have a boundless fascination with water. Exuberant, splashing water play has an obvious appeal on hot summer days, but more measured experimental games are no less enjoyable. During this play, which allows the exploration, however unconsciously, of the properties of water, children learn about sinking and floating, volumes and displacement and the movement of waves and ripples. A creative provision for this type of fun adds greatly to the entertainment value of a children's garden. Ornamental features which have no expanse of open water are safer for areas where children play. However, they are seldom designed with play in mind. Children may enjoy the sensual pleasures of the sound of water and holding their hands in the water's flow, but they have no real play value.

The projects outlined here are specifically designed with play in mind. However, in providing any opportunity for playing with water, safety considerations should be paramount. Carefully consider the ages and capabilities of the children who play in the garden and always provide adequate supervision (see page 156).

Water Serpent • Seaside Wall Fountain • Rill • Bubbling Spring

water serpent

Curled around a hefty bamboo pole, this sinuous yellow and green serpent is an ideal playfellow for hot days. Cooling jets of water spurt from its open mouth, providing the opportunity for some really boisterous water play. As it is supported by firmly pushing the bamboo pole in the ground, the snake is a temporary treat which can be moved all around the garden (as far as the hose will permit). Though it takes very little time to create, the spitting snake is a guaranteed success, as it relentlessly ejects showers of refreshing water on to excited children.

materials
short length of 3.75cm (1¹/₂in)
   bore hose
4m (12ft) of 5cm (2in) bore hose
short length of 2.5cm (1in) bore
   hose
hose connectors
garden hose
silicone sealant or waterproof tape
enamel paint
rubber walking stick end
large bamboo pole
thick twine

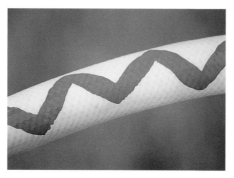

1 Push the 3.75cm (1¹/₂in) bore hose into the end of the thick hose and the 2.5cm (1in) bore hose into that. Then use standard hose attachments to connect this to the garden hose. If necessary, joints can be sealed with silicone sealant or waterproof tape.

2 Using quick-drying enamel paint, decorate the hose with a zigzag pattern along its length. Fortunately this hose already has a texture reminiscent of a snake's scaly skin.

3 Cut a snake-like head into the free end of the large hose using a sharp knife. Pierce holes into the walking stick end and force it into the mouth. Seal around it with silicone sealant.

Adjusting the flow

4 Cut the end of a substantial bamboo pole to form a point. Push the pole into position on the lawn. Twine the serpent around the pole, securing it with thick twine as it crosses the pole. Once the sealant is dry, attach the serpent to the hose.

Take time to create a good arc of water. Ensure that the pressure will not propel the walking stick end from the snake's mouth.

47

seaside wall fountain

Evocative of sunny days on the beach, this brightly coloured wall fountain brings the sound and sparkle of splashing water to even the smallest space. Children are enthralled by the flow of the water, which spills from the top pot into the second and third, and ends up in the bottom pot, from where it is pumped back up to the top. The moving water creates a soothing sound in the garden, which is useful for masking unwanted noises from outside. Painted terracotta wall pots form the cascade, shells and ceramic starfish create a seaside feel. Use a qualified electrician to provide a safe electrical supply with a circuit breaker.

materials

a sheet of 18mm (^{3}/$_4$in)
   exterior-grade plyboard
PVA primer
3 small terracotta wall pots
1 large terracotta wall pot
yellow ceramic tiles
exterior tile adhesive
   and grout
acrylic paints
stainless steel bolts
ceramic starfish
strong glue
electric pond pump
wire mesh
shells

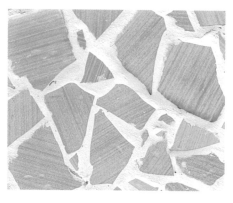

1 Coat the plyboard with a solution of one part PVA to one part water. Allow to dry. Arrange the three small pots and the larger one on the board so that water can flow out of the top one and down through the others.

2 Mark their positions and mark the area for the mosaic sun. Drill an 18mm (³/₄in) hole behind the top pot and behind the lowest pot, for the water pipe to thread through. Drill holes to bolt each wall pot to the board.

3 Create the mosaic sun using broken ceramic tiles and exterior tile adhesive and grout. (See pages 38–39 for details of the mosaic technique.)

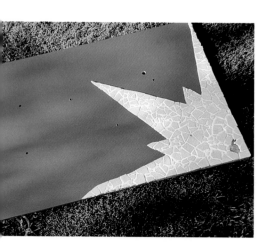

4 Paint the rest of the board with blue acrylic paint, painting carefully around the mosaic. Also paint the terracotta pots in bright colours and them allow to dry.

5 Drill an 18mm (³/₄in) hole in the back of the top wall pot and in the larger one, for the water pipe to thread through. Attach the pots to the board using stainless steel bolts. Glue the starfish into place. Place the pump in the bottom pot and push the cable through the drilled hole to the back of the board.

6 Attach the water pipe to the pump, pass it out of the lower hole up the back of the board and in through the hole behind the top pot. Fill the bottom reservoir with water. Test and adjust the flow of the water through the cascade. Once satisfied, secure wire mesh over the pump and fill the reservoir with shells.

rill

This sophisticated flowing stream has a stylish contemporary feel. Small boats rush from one end to the other, sticks and corks bob along on the current and, on a warm day, it is wide enough for a cooling paddle or a good splash. The dangers of water, however, should never be forgotten. The water in the rill can be kept very shallow, making it safe for older children but younger children will require supervision. It is made from reclaimed RSJs (rolled steel joists) and the water is simply circulated by a pump hidden in a reservoir at the bottom end. A flat garden is not a problem – a drop of only a few centimetres combined with the force of the pump will do the trick. Deceptively straightforward to construct, it requires no special skills. It is prudent to employ a qualified electrician to fit an outside power source for the pump.

materials
2 RSJs, each 4m (12ft) long
rust-proof metal paint
plastic dustbin
fine-gauge wire mesh
silicone sealant
electric pond pump
brick
mosaic paving slab (see pages 38–39)
hardcore
cement
large plain paving slab

1 The two RSJs are butted together to form the rill. When buying reclaimed RSJs take care to ensure that they are straight and that the ends are as neat as possible, as they are often damaged during demolition. Using a wire brush, remove any loose rust and debris then paint them with a rust-proof metal paint.

2 Put the RSJs into position, mark along their edges using a spade and mark the position for the sump (dustbin) at the bottom end, ensuring that the end of the RSJ protrudes over the edge of the sump. Attach a piece of wire mesh across the end of the RSJ to prevent things falling into the sump. Remove the RSJs and dig a shallow trench to house them, so that the top edges are flush with the ground.

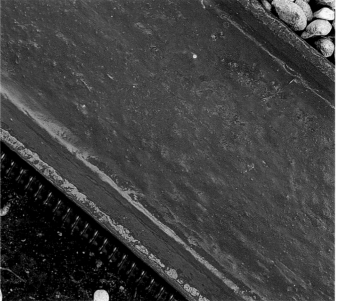

3 Dig a hole for the sump. Fit the RSJs and dustbin into position. You can now check the flow of water along the RSJs using a hose, and adjust the levels if necessary. Remember the pump will provide momentum. Carefully seal the join between the RSJs with a silicone sealant.

4 Place the pump in the dustbin, sitting it on a brick to keep it clear of any debris in the sump. Fit the water pipe to the pump. Run it along the rill to the other end in a small trench, which can be covered over. At the top end of the rill the water pipe should lay 10cm (4in) into the RSJ.

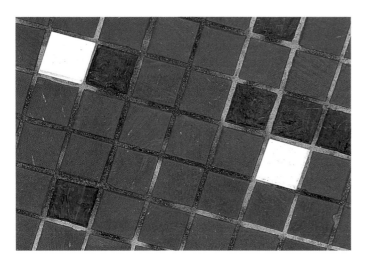

5 A mosaic paving slab forms the capping at the top end of the rill. Dig out a small area around each end of the rill, the correct size for your chosen paving stones, add a layer of hardcore and cement the stones into place. This will hold the water pipe in place at the top of the rill.

6 The sump at the bottom end of the rill can be covered using a large plain paving stone, which can then be covered with gravel or a material which suits the location. Fill the sump with water and connect the pump to the electrical supply.

Getting the balance right

Before finally placing the lid over the sump, adjust the flow of water until the perfect combination of sound and movement is achieved. A few small plastic boats will provide hours of amusement.

Right *Here the colourful rill is located in an area of gravel, but it could be built into a patio, an area of decking or even run through a lawn.*

bubbling spring

Hidden below a vibrant blue square of play matting is an ingenious and versatile water feature. Generally it remains unobtrusive, just the relaxing sound of moving water indicating its presence. When required, jets of water spurt through the blue matting, making it a fantastic place to cool off on a hot day. Though unusual, this feature is completely practical – when the water is kept below the matting its sound can be heard throughout the garden, while the appealingly textured rubber matting provides a warm and welcoming surface. When permitted to burst through, the fine jets of water are irresistible. The matting has a non-slip surface, making play safer, and the water can freely drain back into the sump. The spring will appeal to children of all ages, whether it is for splashing in, lying on, experimenting with or simply cooling off hot feet.

materials
4m (12ft) of 18mm ($^3/_4$in) wide timber
rigid pebble pond liner
white aggregate
electric pond pump and spray nozzles
white cobbles
100cm (36in) square of steel walkway
blue metal paint
4 play matting tiles, each 50cm
    (20in) square

1 Create a rigid timber framework 100cm (36in) square and 15cm (6in) deep in the chosen location. Line the frame with 18mm ($^3/_4$in) wide timber to provide a rim to support the steel mesh and play matting so that the surface of the matting is flush with the top of the frame. Dig a hole at the centre of the frame and set in a pebble pond, ensuring it is level. Dress the soil with white aggregate.

2 Set the pump in the base of the pond. Fill the sump with water and check the flow of the pump before continuing. Put the top on the pond and cover it with white cobbles.

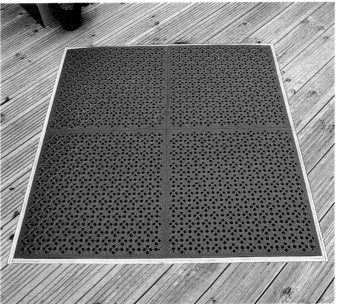

3 Paint the steel walkway using a blue metal paint. Alternatively, use galvanized steel. Fit it into the frame. Link the four play matting tiles together and remove any unwanted lugs.

4 Place the matting on top of the grill. Now the spring is complete. Adjust the flow by using different attachments on the pump's outlet. Lift the matting and add a spray nozzle to send the water spurting through the rubber. Remove the spray nozzle and the water stays out of reach.

growing things

Growing the simplest flowers from seed gives children a sense of pride and a valuable insight into exactly what is required to make plants grow. With just a little more effort and imagination, children can experience growing real food, which can be enjoyed at family meals. Many fruits and vegetables will happily grow in containers, making the task more manageable. It is worth noting that even the fussiest of eaters is invariably happy to consume the fruits of their own labours.

Another significant way in which children can enjoy and explore plants is through the senses. Children will relish the opportunity to smell and taste herbs, instinctively they will explore tactile barks and grasses and derive great satisfaction from popping open flower buds or puncturing fleshy leaves with their nails. It is important to be realistic – children's horticulture is not about striving for the largest yield possible, nor is it about growing the perfect plant. It is about learning through the relaxed enjoyment of growing plants. Children will joyfully plant seeds, water copiously and harvest eagerly, but there will be days when horticultural tasks are not appealing.

Carnivorous Bog • Favourite Herbs • Seed Sowing • Strawberry Tower • Pots of Potatoes • Indoor Hyacinths

carnivorous bog

Create an acid bog in any watertight container and it provides the perfect growing conditions for fascinating carnivorous plants. The macabre characteristics of these plants are immediately attractive to children, who are at once both entranced and repulsed by their ingenious insect-trapping techniques. Many, such as sarracenias (pitcher plants), have an architectural beauty while their flowers are relatively insignificant but beguilingly pretty.

Despite their exotic appearance, most carnivorous plants are straightforward to grow given the right conditions. Many are hardy when grown in a sheltered spot and require no feeding as all their nutrition comes from the insects they trap. They do, however, require copious amounts of rainwater – not tap water as this has a high lime content. The plants chosen here are natives of acid bogs, many of them under threat in their native habitats.

materials
wooden wine case or other container
red acrylic paint
thick polythene
peat
lime-free horticultural sand
carnivorous plants, such as *Sarracenia
    flava*, *Sarracenia purpurea purpurea*,
    Dionaea muscipula and *Drosera*
black glass mulch

1 Choose a container for the bog garden. Here a wooden wine case is painted a dramatic red which sets off the plants beautifully.

2 If the container is not watertight, line it with thick polythene.

3 Half-fill the container with a mixture of six parts peat to one part sand. Sadly in this instance there is no viable alternative to peat, but ensure the peat you buy is from a site of no scientific interest. Firm down the mixture and roughly level the surface.

4 Arrange the plants in the container and move them around until a pleasing combination of shapes, colours and forms is achieved. A large number of plants will create instant impact, but you could use fewer plants and wait for them to grow and fill the box.

5 Traditionally, carnivorous plants are mulched with sphagnum moss for a natural appearance. Here black glass mulch has been used to finish off this show-stopping container. This glass mulch is safe to handle, but as a precaution you could wear gloves.

6 Now soak the container with rainwater. Keep it in a sunny, sheltered position, ensuring it is always well watered with rainwater.

Choosing plants for the bog

Right *The box has been painted to match an area of the garden with red border edgings and red flowers. It stands on a path of black glass mulch.*

Far left and centre left *Sarracenias exude irresistible nectar around the rim of their funnel-shaped leaves to attract flies, wasps and other insects. Once on the plant, they lose their grip on the slippery sides of the pitcher and drop into the trap. Some sarracenias have pitchers 90cm (36in) tall.*

Left **Drosera** *(sundews) are smaller plants whose leaves are covered with vibrant red hairs. These secrete shining, sticky spheres which hold its prey fast while it is digested.*

favourite herbs

Exploring the taste, texture and scent of culinary herbs can be a thrilling experience for a child – the fresh smell of mint, the pungent taste of chives and the smooth leather of bay leaves which, once cracked, release their subtle aroma. Allow children to experiment and choose their favourites to grow in a large container. Alternatively, try growing a collection of herbs for a favourite dish; for example basil, marjoram and garlic for pasta dishes. Most herbs are undemanding plants and will make prodigious growth with very little care and attention, making them an ideal choice for the young horticulturalist.

materials

4 or 5 herb plants
terracotta container
yellow acrylic paint
crocks
multipurpose compost
horticultural grit
wooden label

1 Allow the children to choose four or five of their favourite herb plants. Encourage them to choose plants that they will enjoy eating.

2 Choose a large container for the herbs. Here an inexpensive terracotta pot has been painted a sunny yellow to set off the fresh herb foliage.

3 Put a layer of crocks in the bottom of the pot and fill it with multipurpose compost, adding a few handfuls of horticultural grit as you go. Carefully remove the herbs from their pots.

4 Carefully plant the herbs, water them in and place the pot in a sunny spot. A large decorative label, made from a wooden plaque and a chopstick, adds a final flourish.

favourite herbs 63

seed sowing

Seed collecting is an absorbing pastime for the days of late summer and early autumn. Children find a great satisfaction in cracking the brittle dried casings and releasing the precious seeds inside, marvelling at their profusion.

The seeds can be easily shaken out into a brown paper envelope, labelled and stored in a cool, dark, dry place until spring, when they can be coaxed into life. Some, such as nigella and aquilegia, can be broadcast immediately, perhaps in the child's special garden, and will obligingly grow where they land.

This simple activity affords a real insight into the almost magical life cycle of plants and ensures that the garden will be brimming with new plants next year.

materials
brown paper bags
seeds
flower pots
multipurpose compost

1 Collect seeds, such as these sunflower seeds, in late summer or autumn. Store them in a brown paper bag in a cool place until spring.

2 Fill some small flower pots with compost and firm it lightly. Push the seeds into the compost, one to a pot, about 2.5cm (1in) deep.

3 Water the pots well to moisten the compost. Stand them in a sunny spot and keep moist until the seedlings appear.

4 When the seedlings are large enough to handle, plant them out in the garden and watch them grow.

strawberry tower

A stack of colourful seaside buckets is a practical and appealing way to produce cascades of shining red strawberries. High-rise growing allows a reasonable crop of strawberries to be produced in the smallest of spaces. Harvest time will be eagerly awaited, the progress of each strawberry keenly observed as the fruit swells and ripens. When the time comes, eating the strawberries straight from the plant, still warm from the sun, is a real delight. By using a mixture of varieties which crop at different times, the harvest can go on all summer long. Keep the plants well watered and feed with a high-potash fertilizer once a month for a really bumper crop.

materials
4 plastic buckets
crocks
multipurpose compost
8 strawberry plants

1 Choose four colourful plastic buckets, graduated in size, and good fruiting varieties of strawberry, such as 'Cambridge Favourite', 'Cambridge Vigour' and 'Red Gauntlet', which crop at different times.

2 Drill drainage holes in the bottom of each of the buckets and add a layer of broken crocks. These will aid drainage and prevent the compost leaching out of the holes in the bottoms of the buckets.

3 Half-fill each bucket with multipurpose compost and stack them up according to size to form the strawberry tower.

4 Fill the spaces between the buckets with more compost, packing it in almost to the rim of each bucket. Firm it down well.

5 Plant strawberry plants around each level and water them in. Eight plants are needed for a tower of this size. Place in a sunny spot.

pots of potatoes

Starting with just a few seed potatoes, a child can experience the excitement of unearthing enough delicious homegrown potatoes for several family meals. The seemingly miraculous multiplication of a handful of tubers into a crop of tasty new potatoes is always a source of great wonderment. Choosing a variety boasting a high yield, disease resistance and suitability for container growing will help guarantee success. The variety chosen here is 'Vanessa'. All that is required is a sunny position, plenty of water and a weekly feed with a liquid fertilizer. The potatoes can be planted as soon as the risk of frost has passed, or slightly earlier if they can be protected from frost in a greenhouse or porch, for example. Care is needed when completing this project with young children, as all parts of the potato plant are toxic.

materials
seed potatoes
large pot
multipurpose compost
plant label

1 Before planting, leave the seed potatoes in a light, frost-free place for several weeks to chit, that is produce sprouts. An egg box makes an ideal container, allowing the tubers to be stood with 'eyes' uppermost – this is where the chits will form. Warmth can hurry along the process. When the chits are about 13mm ($^{1}/_{2}$in) long, they are ready to plant.

2 Choose a deep pot with holes for drainage and put a layer of compost, about 15cm (6in) deep, in the base. A 40cm (16in) pot can accommodate three or four seed potatoes. Place the potatoes on the compost, shoot ends up, and cover with another 10cm (4in) of compost, firming it down. Water well.

3 Label the pot. This chunky, painted label provides plenty of space to record the variety planted. Soon shoots will appear. When they reach 20cm (8in) they require 'earthing up'.

4 This means building up soil around the shoots, leaving half the growth showing. This is a weekly task until the top of the pot is reached. Water the compost well each time.

5 The harvest is always eagerly awaited. Early potatoes are usually ready when they flower. Carefully loosen the root and pull out the buried treasures.

indoor hyacinths

With some forward planning during the darker days of autumn, a little of the colour and scent of spring can be persuaded to arrive early. Using any glass container and vividly coloured aquatic gravels, florist's beads, pebbles, buttons, shells, plastic beads or even plastic figures, children can create their own decorative containers in which hyacinth bulbs can grow. The beautiful finished pots make a thoughtful homemade gift. Be sure to choose hyacinth bulbs which are suitable for forcing.

materials
hyacinth bulbs
glass beads and shapes
colourful aquatic gravels
glass containers

1 The purple-skinned bulbs of the hyacinth 'Blue Jacket' are excellent for forcing. The shoots will emerge from the top, pointed end of the bulb.

2 Iridescent blue moons and stars with contrasting bright yellow aquatic gravel will show off the blue of the hyacinth blooms when they come into flower.

3 Fill a glass vase with the gravel, arranging the stars or decorations as you go. Here is the chance to let the children use their creativity with their chosen fillings.

Watering

Keep the water level topped up so that it stays in contact with the bases of the bulbs until the roots are well established.

4 Sit the bulbs on the top and fill with water to the bottom of the bulbs. Add a few more glass beads around the bulbs.

5 Put in a cool dark place until the emerging shoots are 2.5–5cm (1–2in) tall. Then they can be put on the windowsill where, no doubt, their progress will be proudly watched.

indoor hyacinths **71**

wildlife and pets

Creating a garden which is a haven for wildlife can be an enriching and exciting experience for children, the majority of whom have few other opportunities to come into contact with native creatures. A garden which is home to bats, frogs, toads, hedgehogs, butterflies, insects and a myriad of wild birds is a stimulating place to play. The chance to observe and nurture the wildlife in the garden builds a child's knowledge and engenders a real interest in and respect for the environment.

Tempting creatures into the garden is not hard – a few simple measures form the groundwork. First, do not use pesticides. Second, create less manicured areas of garden and permit a little decay. Third, grow shrubs and plants which provide nectar, seeds and berries for food. Add a few features specifically designed to encourage wildlife and the animal and insect population in the garden should rapidly increase.

Keeping a family pet affords a different set of experiences, helping children to learn responsibility for others, and develop their nurturing skills. This chapter also includes two projects designed to make that experience more enjoyable.

Pet Palace • Wildlife Container Pond • Rustic Bird Feeder • Catmint Cat Basket

pet palace

Housing for small pets is usually at best drab, fit only for the furthest reaches of the garden. This pet palace, with its exotic decoration and vibrant colours, offers a stunning alternative. Suitable for guinea pigs and rabbits, it is not only stylish but it is very practical. It combines a cosy weatherproof bed box, with a well-protected, spacious run. Cleaning out is an easy task. If the pet is in the habit of burrowing, add a mesh floor, which will still allow access to the grass but prevent an escape. Using trellis panels and recycling wooden wine cases makes construction straightforward and economical; only the most rudimentary of carpentry skills are needed.

materials

3 trellis panels 2mx60cm (6ftx24in)
non-toxic wood-preserving stain
5 pieces of 5cm (2in) square timber,
    60cm (24in) long
galvanized wire mesh and staples
galvanized screws
2 galvanized hinges
5 safety hooks and eyes
2 wine cases
wood filler
2 fretwork strips, 60cm (24in) long
wood glue
plastic tray
scrap wood for ramp
wooden finials

1 Sand the three trellis panels and treat them with wood stain. This vibrant blue looks fantastic against the green of the grass. Sand and stain the rest of the timber to match.

2 Cut two of the trellis panels into two, giving one piece 120cm (48in) long and the other 60cm (24in) long – these will form the sides of the run. Use four pieces of 5cm (2in) timber to form the corner posts.

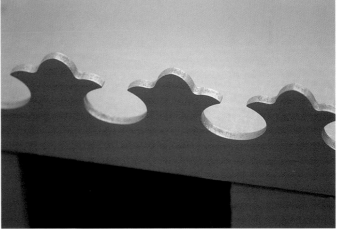

3 Tack galvanized mesh on to the insides of the four side panels, securing it with wire staples. Screw the panels together to form a rectangular run, securing a post at each corner. Use one of the smaller panels to form the gate, hinged from one of the corner posts. Use the fifth piece of 5cm (2in) timber to form a threshold at the bottom of the gate to add rigidity. Secure the gate with a safety hook and eye.

4 To make the bed box, cut a door in one of the wine cases (these are a waste product of wine importers) and cut down the other to form a lid. Fill any cracks with wood filler to make it weatherproof. Use wood glue to stick the strip of fretwork to the front of the lid and finish off with a matching coat of preservative.

Right *Perhaps one of the best features of this pet palace is that the children can get into the run with their pets, closing the door behind them, so the pets are still safe and secure inside the run.*

5 Screw the box into the back of the run, raised above the ground to keep it dry. A plastic tray in the bottom of the box makes cleaning out easy. Use a scrap of wood to construct a ramp. Cut the remaining piece of trellis to fit the top of the run. Tack mesh on to its underside and add a strip of fretwork to the front. A pair of oversized finials, glued to the top of the lid, adds a final flourish. Safety hooks and eyes can be used to hold the top in place.

Scaling up

With luck, your pet guinea pigs and rabbits will be part of the family for six or seven years, so it is worth creating a special residence for them. This basic design can be scaled up to accommodate greater numbers of pets or larger breeds.

wildlife container pond

This handsome container pond may be small but it gives children the opportunity to observe aquatic wildlife and insects. The pond is quick to create and looks at home nestled into any garden border. The aquatic plants chosen here are particularly valuable for attracting insects – those who prey on them will also be encouraged. The large blue glazed pot complements the blues and whites of the aquatic plants' flowers and echoes the planting around it. In gardens for younger children, the top of the pond should be protected with firmly secured rigid steel mesh.

materials
large waterproof glazed pot
silicone sealant (optional)
bricks
aquatic plants
cobbles
dragonfly decoration

1 Choose a large glazed pot. If the base is unglazed, seal it with silicone sealant to make it waterproof. Set the pot into the ground, leaving about 10cm (4in) above the ground, and ensure that the pot is level.

2 Arrange bricks in the base of the pond to support the plant pots, so that the surface of the compost will be approximately 15cm (6in) below the surface of the water. Fill the pot with water.

3 Choose relatively small-growing aquatic plants for the container, such as *Ranunculus aquatilis*, *Glyceria maxima variegata*, *Mentha cervina*, *Gratiola officinalis* and *Nasturtium aquaticum*. Gently lower the plants into position. Using this number of plants gives instant impact but fewer would soon fill the space.

4 Ensure that frogs and toads can get in and out of the pond easily, by arranging large cobbles around its edge, and placing others just below the surface of the water. A shining brass and copper dragonfly hovering among the plants is a fitting adornment for the pond.

rustic bird feeder

Watching the birds which visit this bird feeder will be all the more rewarding as the children can make a real contribution to its construction. This simple alternative to the traditional bird table is quick and easy to make, with plenty of tasks to interest the children. As well as providing much-needed food for small birds, such as blue tits, finches and nuthatches, it makes an attractive addition to gardens with a rustic feel.

materials

large branch
terracotta pot
ready-mix concrete
fir cones
thick twine
wire
fat balls
peanuts
windfall apples
seed bells
rose hips

1 Chose a suitable branch and trim it, leaving a stout framework with a pleasing shape.

2 Concrete the branch into a large terracotta pot for stability. When the concrete is dry, dress the top of the pot with fir cones.

3 Thread and tie fat balls, peanuts, windfall apples and seed bells on to wire and thick twine to arrange on the branch.

Food for the bird feeder

Clusters of rose hips, fir cones and big bows of shaggy rustic twine decorate the edible treats attached to the bird feeder. Replace the food as the birds eat it, using whatever you have to hand – berries, seedheads and kitchen scraps are all welcome.

catmint cat basket

Cats will adore this basket, planted with irresistible catmint. Its humour is instantly appealing, while it is simple enough for older children to create and maintain with little supervision. It is the smell of the catmint that cats find so alluring. As they roll on the plants, crushing the leaves and stems, the fragrance is released. This rolling can be quite damaging to the plants, so give the catmint a chance to establish before presenting this gift to the cat – and perhaps restrict access for a while if the damage becomes too great. Nepeta (catmint) is a fast-growing plant and not only should it provide the cat with endless pleasure, it will produce a haze of pretty blue flowers above soft grey foliage all summer long.

materials
wicker basket
5 nepeta plants
exterior matt varnish
thick polythene
crocks
multipurpose compost
horticultural grit
slate mulch

1 Choose a small wicker cat basket and five or six plants of either *Nepeta cataria* or *Nepeta* x *faassenii*, the varieties of catmint which are most preferred by cats.

2 Coat the basket inside and out with a good layer of varnish to help prevent rot and line the inside of it with polythene sheeting. Make a few drainage holes in the polythene and add a layer of crocks.

3 Half-fill the basket with compost, mixed with a few handfuls of grit, and pack it up round the sides to form a dip in the middle. Plant the nepeta around the outside of the basket.

4 Adding a layer of slate mulch over the bare compost sets the plants off beautifully and gives the cat a firm surface to sleep on. Finally water the basket well. Catmint, like cats, prefers a warm sunny spot.

celebrations

The garden provides the perfect setting for childhood celebrations, as exuberant revellers can be afforded greater freedom away from the restrictions of carpets and soft furnishings. Decorating a garden for the occasion makes it a more exciting place, transforming the space from the familiar to the extraordinary – setting the scene for something special. The decorative materials do not have to be lavish or expensive, but rather imaginative and well chosen. Many things children can design and make themselves. The more unexpected or complete the transformation, the more exciting the effect will be. Often a trawl through drawers, cupboards and sheds will produce a lot of promising raw materials.

At times when the weather is inclement, decorating just part of the garden can create a magnificent entrance as guests arrive. On view through windows during the party, these scenes contribute to the special ambience. Even if most of the celebrations are held inside, the garden is the ideal location for energetic games, allowing excited guests the freedom to let off steam. Preparing for celebrations takes time, but can be just as much fun as the event itself. The extra effort put into creating a landscape for the party or celebration is well worthwhile and goes a long way to making it an occasion to remember. Encourage children to take part in the planning – they will undoubtedly have ideas about the design and arrangement of decorations.

Easter Egg Hunt • Midsummer Party • Halloween • Christmas
• Party Gifts

easter
egg hunt

For most families, Easter celebrations include a hunt for chocolate Easter eggs for the children. Dashing around the garden and rummaging through shrubs and plants searching for the hidden chocolate treasures is great fun. Decorate the garden for the occasion and the hunt becomes very special indeed.

Easter decorations add excitement, movement and colour to the garden; the fresh greens and yellows echo the colours prevalent in the spring-time garden. The decorations, though simple, change the garden from the familiar and everyday to an exciting place for revelry and fun. Best of all, the planning and preparation for the hunt provide plenty of opportunity for the children to use their creative talents.

Above *Swathed in fresh yellow silk ribbons and hung with tiny painted wooden eggs, a clipped* Ligustrum *(privet) bush provides the centrepiece for the party.*

Right *Polystyrene eggs decorated by the children using acrylic paints are mounted on bamboo skewers to make cheerful decorations.*

Far right *Making small parcels of chocolate eggs wrapped in clear plastic and tied with ribbons helps keep them clean and dry. Use different coloured ribbon for each child so everyone gets their fair share of the spoils.*

Above *Personalizing colourful dyed eggs makes a fun addition to afternoon tea. To make them, first hard-boil some eggs. When they are cool, draw on a design using a white crayon or a candle. Next make a solution of half a bottle of food colouring, 300ml (½ pint) of water, 2 tablespoons of vinegar and a tablespoon of salt. Dip the eggs into the mixture and leave them until the desired colour is achieved.*

Left *Yellow and green banners add height and movement to the garden. These are made from pieces of sheeting stitched together, with a sleeve stitched down the long edge. They are simply threaded on to garden canes. Inexpensive baskets with yellow and green bows are ideal for egg collecting. Each child can decorate their own before the hunt.*

How to dye eggs

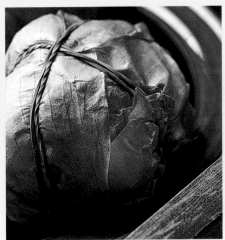

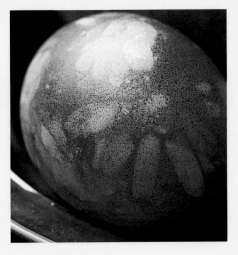

1 Traditionally, in many parts of Europe, eggs are dyed using flowers and leaves. Collect flowers and foliage from the garden.

2 Arrange the flowers and leaves around the raw egg and wrap in onion skins. Secure with elastic bands and hard-boil the eggs.

3 When cool, remove the wrapping to reveal the surprising patterns beneath. These eggs are for decorative purposes only.

Above *After an afternoon of hunting eggs and chasing around the garden, an alfresco Easter tea is much appreciated.*

Right *Shaped cutters and a little yellow icing make these basic homemade biscuits especially appealing.*

Above *Cheery purple violas make a perfect centrepiece for the tea table. Chicks on sticks add a touch of Easter fun.*

Right *A splash of green acrylic paint transforms a flower pot into a container for an abundance of chocolate eggs.*

Top *Give any small cake extra appeal with a topping of foil-wrapped chocolate eggs.*

Above *The Simnel cake is an essential part of any Easter tea.*

midsummer party

Party planning and preparations provide an excellent diversion for the long holidays. To make this summer party more of an occasion, the most unassuming garden feature, the lawn, takes centre stage – careful mowing produces the game board for the party. This ingenuous effect requires some forward planning: leave the lawn unmown for a week or two, depending on the growing conditions. Then, after marking out the proposed layout with ropes or canes, mow away sections of the lawn leaving areas of contrasting long grass which define the games. A little imagination can produce more than enough activities for an afternoon of fun.

Right *All sorts of races, like the egg and spoon race, are wonderfully exciting and use up masses of energy.*

Far right *The garden provides the ideal setting for the boisterous fun of excited party revellers.*

Below *As well as the mown lanes for the races, an array of mown paths meander through another part of the garden, criss-crossing each other and making an unpredictable selection of routes. This is an ideal area for impromptu chasing games and letting off steam.*

Right *Boule is an absorbing, almost compulsive game, which can be enjoyed by all ages, as they compete on an equal footing. It is usually played on gravel or sand, but here a court is mown into the lawn, its boundary emphasized with bright sunflower heads laid on the grass. Defining the area of the game in this way is not only appealing, it also prevents play from straying into other more boisterous activities.*

Below *All sorts of races can be run in this set of mown parallel lanes. Novelty races, such as egg and spoon or crawling backwards races, are fun and a great leveller allowing all ages to compete together. Children can devise their own programme of races and events. To help things run smoothly, have all the props needed ready at the starting line.*

Above and top *The relaxed informality of a picnic tea is suited to this kind of party. A few simple touches, such as decorative place markers and table decorations, make it feel special.*

Above and right *An unremarkable birdbath, given a touch of glamour with florist's beads and silver paint, provides the very remarkable centrepiece for the grassy game board. Filled with bubble mixture and floating flowers, it is irresistible. Set challenges to prolong the amusement – get the children to try blowing the largest bubble, catching the most bubbles, or perhaps the longest stream of bubbles in one single breath.*

Left *A shady place to eat and cool off is important after an afternoon of energetic fun. The shade canopy makes an ideal shelter, creating an intimate space in which to eat and rest.*

Below left *The luscious colours of berries in a sumptuous ice bowl makes a perfect centrepiece. Children can make the ice bowl the day before the party, picking snippets of herbs and edible flowers and arranging them in an ice bowl mould. Alternatively, use one bowl set inside another, in which you have already frozen a small amount of water to form the base. When packed with flowers, fill the mould with water and freeze overnight. To release the ice bowl from the mould simply dip it into some lukewarm water and gently work it loose.*

Below *A fragrant bunch of herbs and flowers tied with a ribbon mark the place of each guest, their name written on the shiny side of a rose leaf.*

▶ see **Shade Canopy**, page 154

midsummer party **97**

halloween

In the twilight of All Hallow's Eve, the glow of grotesquely carved pumpkins, the silhouette of a hook-nosed witch and the flickering flames of huge torches create a bewitching scene to greet party guests.

This small courtyard was dressed to provide a suitably ghostly atmosphere when guests arrived for a children's Halloween party. The area also played host to a number of party games. As darkness falls, the eerie glow of pumpkin lanterns can be seen through the window adding to the feeling of mystery and magic. All the usual elements of Halloween are here, but none of the ghastly gore. Carving pumpkins, cutting out bats and reorganizing the garden takes some time, but children will enjoy making the props almost as much as they enjoy the party.

Burning candles and fires are a safety hazard. Take care that children are never left unsupervised around lit candles and fires and that all candles are securely placed and not left unattended.

Above and above right *Grouping pumpkins together gives them more impact. Lanterns burn alongside some rather more curious ones which have sprouted hair. Carving the face into the surface of the pumpkin means they can be planted with grasses. Here the ornamental grasses* Uncinia rubra *and* Ophiopogon planiscapus *'Nigrescens' have been used. Safely out of children's reach, huge flares have a gothic feel.*

Right *Halloween celebrations are one of the best opportunities for dressing up, even for grown ups.*

Above *The traditional game of apple bobbing is great fun, but messy and best played outside.*

Left *A host of shining bats cut from thick black polythene adorns windows, walls, plants, trellis and trees.*

Above *The window is dressed with carved pumpkin lanterns, black polythene bats, twisted twigs, silvery stars and black fabric to make a sinister backdrop.*

Above right *The leaping flames and sparks of this wrought-iron brazier, set at a safe distance, adds real drama to the scene.*

Right *These glowing lanterns are quick and simple to make. Draw a design on coloured tissue paper and cut out unwanted areas to create the design. Wrap the pieces of tissue paper around the outsides of empty jam jars, securing them with sticky tape, and add a night light.*

Above *This striking silhouette of a hook-nosed witch and her bubbling cauldron is cut from thick black polythene (black pond liner is excellent for this). Set against the light-coloured background, lit by lanterns, the scene becomes more eerie at twilight. This striking decoration can easily be rolled up and brought out again for next year's celebrations.*

Right *Children unable to take part in carving pumpkins can still contribute by designing their grotesque faces in marker pen on the skin for an adult to cut out.*

christmas

At this time of year when all else is joyful and sparkling, the garden is often forgotten. Bringing some of the colour and glamour of Christmas into the garden can provide a wonderful diversion for excited children. It is pleasant to look out on a festive scene or provide a special welcome for Christmas visitors.

The front door is an obvious place to start with the decorations, and then perhaps choose to decorate the areas most viewed from the house. If the children have a place of their own in the garden, then this can be prepared for the festive season too. Many ready-made Christmas decorations can be used outside, but it is much more rewarding for children to create their own.

Above *Decorating your own place in the garden just the way you want it and with decorations you have made yourself is great fun and an achievement worth showing off.*

Above right *A wreath of twigs is adorned with striped candy canes.*

Right *Christmas trees cut from craft foam and vibrant green beads on bead wire form a garland along the roofline.*

Left *A twinkling welcome for visitors comes from lanterns cut from silver card, covering tea lights. (Children should not play with lit candles, these lanterns should not be left unattended.)*

Below left *This summerhouse has been decorated using silver and purple home-made decorations. Pots of twisted willow twigs, sprayed silver, are given extra sparkle with strings of plastic beads threaded on to bead wire. A swathe of silver star confetti sweeps across its entire facade. A large twig wreath, sprayed silver with a bold purple bow, adorns the door. The lights add extra glamour and sparkle at twilight.*

Below *Silver stars are applied to the outside of the summerhouse using temporary fixings which can easily be removed after Christmas.*

Top left *Lavishly studded with shining wrapped sweets, this wreath has obvious child appeal. It is easy to make; the sweets are simply pinned on to a polystyrene ring using florist's wire, bent into hairpin shapes.*

Top right *At this time when festive fare abounds, it is easy to forget the wild birds in the garden. They may not appreciate the festive trappings but they will certainly welcome the food on offer.*

Bottom left *Even the youngest child can produce these simple bead drops.*

Bottom right *Flower pot angels, fashioned from raffia and terracotta pots with a hint of gold paint, are a delightful naive decoration for a garden gate or potting shed.*

Left *Here, bead drops hang on a twisted willow decoration, but they could be used to adorn any tree or shrub. Simply tie them in place.*

Below left and below *Fat balls and peanuts can be hung from all sorts of decorative contraptions of beads, buttons and baubles, creating a really bright spot in the winter garden.*

party gifts

Containers of flowering plants make welcome gifts for any occasion. Deliciously fragrant violas, planted in a decorated box, make a very special gift which is well suited to birthdays or Mother's day. The simple stamping used to create the painted design is quick and easy for children of all ages. The finished box looks good on an outdoor windowsill, or as a centrepiece for a garden table. Alternatively, plant a single plant in a decorated pot for a quick and easy gift. The Valentine's pot is enchantingly simple, an ideal gift for childhood sweethearts.

materials

wooden port gift box
purple acrylic paint
large potato
gold acrylic paint
thick polythene
crocks
multipurpose compost
6 viola plants

1 Remove any internal divisions from the box and drill a few holes in the base. Paint the box using acrylic paint.

2 Cut the pattern to be stamped from half of a large potato. Children can design the stamp to be cut out by an adult.

3 Pour a little gold paint on to a saucer and dip the stamp into it to coat the surface.

Valentine's pots

4 Print the pattern on to the box. Here a luxurious combination of gold and rich purple has been used. Line the box with polythene, making holes in the base, and plant with six small violas spaced evenly in the box.

These are basic terracotta pots painted with yellow acrylic paint. Add a scalloped band of red at the top of the pot. Allow the paint to dry and plant the pot with a scarlet primula.

Stick shining red glass hearts on to the pot using PVA primer and stick glass hearts on painted bamboo skewers to make a decoration. Push the bamboo skewers into the compost in the pot.

finishing touches

Decorative details can really enhance a garden – they embellish its structure, bringing colour, atmosphere and perhaps humour. This is no less true in a garden for children, where carefully chosen finishing touches can provide a feast for the senses with their sound, colour and light. The style of the pieces chosen will affect the ambience of the garden, giving it a distinctive personality. Placed with care, decorative details provide points of interest in the garden to delight the eye.

The appreciation of these details is very much a personal matter. Often bits and pieces with a personal history or objets trouvés make wonderful adornments, while a collection of mundane objects creatively grouped together can form a stunning still life. A deftly applied coat of paint transforms the everyday into the decorative. Basic criteria can be applied when choosing finishing touches. The rules to follow are: is it enjoyed by the children? And does it sit comfortably in the garden?

Children can be encouraged to take part in adorning their own garden, creating their own touches to make the garden a personal space, a gallery in which achievements can displayed.

Customizing Pots • Mobiles and Chimes • Buying Finishing Touches

customizing pots

Flower pots, troughs and containers are perfect for customizing. For example, colourfully painted pots with frames to match are marvellously decorative. The ornate frames give emphasis and glamour to horticultural triumphs. Children can create their own pots and frames and use them to exhibit their prize plants. Simple wooden frames sealed with PVA primer can be decorated with a myriad of techniques, from a coat of acrylic paint to mosaic, to produce a wide range of designs.

Alternatively, bring a touch of humour into the garden with some amusing portrait pots. Each child can chose to paint themselves or a family member. Planting the pot with ornamental grass 'hair' completes the picture; there are grasses with many different habits, colours and textures, so there is bound to be one to suit everyone.

Above and top *Basic wooden wine boxes make fine planters which can be decorated to suit their location and the types of plants they house. Drill a few drainage holes in the bases and paint with acrylic paints. Line the boxes with black polythene and puncture a few holes in the bottom before filling with compost and planting up.*

Left and far left *Paint the portrait pots using a flesh-toned masonry paint, then use acrylics to paint the faces. Perhaps paint one on each side – happy and sad, or asleep and awake. These pots are planted with the rust-coloured* Carex comans *bronze form, black ophiopogon and yellow variegated* Acorus gramineus *to form the hair.*

Left and far left
A pink and violet frame adorned with coloured gravels draws attention to the flowers of this sunny yellow plant.

Left and far left
A shell encrusted sky-blue pot with matching frame is ideal for the fleshy leaves of Aeonium balsamiferum.

mobiles and chimes

Mobile-making is one of the easiest projects; even a very young child can make a real contribution as soon as they can thread beads. For an afternoon of creative fun, provide a selection of raw materials and stand by to assist with any tricky knot tying. Anything which will withstand the elements can be strung to provide colour, movement, light and sound. Beads, fir cones, shells, small plastic figures or even cutlery are all possibilities. Suspend them using durable nylon thread and bead wire or, for a more rustic chunky look, opt for a thick hairy twine.

Above *Strings of carefully chosen plastic beads contrast beautifully with the gleaming bark of the betula (silver birch) and pick up the colour of the summerhouse behind.*

Left *Making mobiles is an enjoyable activity for children of all ages. Supply plenty of twine, nylon thread, beads, shells, fir cones, sticks and any other items that can be threaded and allow the children to hang up the mobiles themselves in the garden.*

Above *Compact discs have a contemporary look. They mirror the colours around them and project flashes of dancing light across the garden as they move in the breeze.*

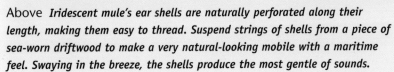

Above *Iridescent mule's ear shells are naturally perforated along their length, making them easy to thread. Suspend strings of shells from a piece of sea-worn driftwood to make a very natural-looking mobile with a maritime feel. Swaying in the breeze, the shells produce the most gentle of sounds.*

Right *Long strands of glass florist's beads shine and sparkle in sunlight. Pairs of glass beads are glued together, sandwiching a length of invisible nylon thread. For the best effect, make long strings and tie them where they can be lit by the sun.*

buying finishing touches

There are many decorative pieces available in shops, a great proportion of which have a real charm, especially when used with wit and intelligence. It is important to select pieces carefully, choosing those which will add to the appeal of the garden rather than detract from it. A brightly coloured piece is unlikely to sit well in a rural location. Similarly, rusticity may look uncomfortable in a garden with a contemporary feel. Many decorative items designed for interior decoration will survive the elements and are worth considering.

Above *Even wildlife can be accommodated stylishly in these contemporary bird boxes. Their vibrant colours and clean lines make them a stunning alternative to more traditional bird boxes.*

Right *The organic simplicity of this beautifully crafted ewe and her lambs has a quiet but inescapable charm, which is not lost on children. Sculptures made from natural materials are the perfect ornament for green gardens or those with an air of rusticity.*

Left and below left *Shoals of sculpted wooden fish look convincing as they swim through the plants in these borders.*

real children's gardens

Designing a garden for children is not an easy task, especially when there is a wide range of ages or interests to accommodate. However, setting aside a portion of the garden and furnishing it with a well-chosen array of stimulating play features is well worth the effort. Children who have an interesting, challenging and well-tailored area for fun in the garden are more likely to play contentedly and gain much more from the experience.

A children's garden should, however, be more than just an assemblage of age-appropriate equipment. With a little effort, disparate features can be woven together to create a magical place whose appeal is far greater than the sum of its parts.

In this chapter, five diverse children's gardens are explored. Each is a response to a different collection of needs and circumstances. None of the gardens is large and each occupies a portion of a larger family garden.

The Crocodile Garden • The Toddler's Play Deck • The Jungle Outpost • The Child-sized Potager • The Relaxing Retreat

the crocodile garden

Once an overgrown vegetable patch, this garden was designed for three children aged nine, six and four. The aim was to create a versatile space which offered something for each of them: props for imaginative games, scope to let off steam and a place to eat and relax. Each of these children had a clear idea of what they wanted from their garden. Features to attract wildlife, a cosy den and a sandpit were deemed essential. Sadly, real hippos wallowing in a water hole proved to be difficult to provide, but a crocodile in the lawn is a great substitute.

This children's garden is separated from the rest of the garden by a leafy living willow trellis, which gives a feeling of privacy and freedom to the children but still allows adults to keep an eye on what is going on.

Above *Setting the trampoline flush with the relatively soft lawn ensures that even the most reckless bouncing does not result in a serious fall.*

Above *A wonderfully gnarled lilac tree, removed from another part of the garden, has been set in concrete and now supports rope swings, colourful planted pots, bird feeders and mobiles.*

Right *Christened the 'guardian of the garden', this crocodile is a mound of well-firmed topsoil, laid over a thin hardcore base, which has then been skillfully turfed. The children sit on him, jump off him and even talk to him. A quick clip twice a week and a water in dry weather will keep the crocodile lush and green.*

Left *A wigwam of willow withies has been grown to form a leafy den. A layer of cocoa shells provides a wonderfully soft, chocolate-scented flooring. Withies (essentially pieces of willow) will root readily when simply pushed into position, but if the ground is poor, incorporate some moisture-retentive material into the soil and keep watered.*

Below left *Large enough for two or even three, this stripy hammock is a great place to relax, read or just gaze skyward. Slung between railway sleeper totem poles, concreted into the ground, the hammock is easy to get into and falling out does not present a hazard.*

Below *A face for each child: railway sleepers painted with acrylic paint, topped with a coat of exterior varnish, support the hammock. Their humorous appearance gives them a decorative value even when not in use.*

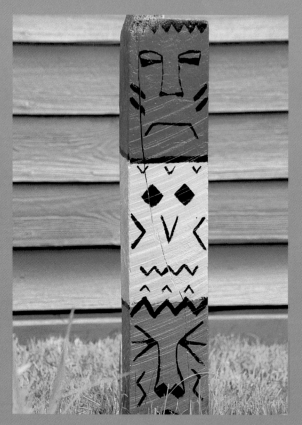

Left *This tiniest of ponds attracted frogs and toads in just a few days. The bright yellow flowers of* Ranunculus lingua, *growing amid the pebbles on the marginal shelf, are shown off against the blue of the decking frame. This frame hides the edges of the pond liner and supports a grill of iron bars so that the children can pond-dip in safety.*

Below left *This hefty oak table echoes the crocodile form in the lawn. Sturdy benches attached along its sides provide enough space for at least ten children. Its stable, robust form shrugs off mistreatment. This bench was made to order by a local carpenter.*

Below *A striking orange viola in a sky blue pot, painted by the children, hangs on the tree.*

Left and below *A large sandpit means disputes over accidentally demolished sand castles are less likely. A salvaged door, painted in blue, makes a sturdy waterproof lid for the sandpit. Stout fastenings hold the lid securely open when the sandpit is in use.*

Left *The rustic gazebo, home to the crocodile bench, is topped with an unusual fish ornament.*

the toddler's play deck

For young children, play is all about having fun. But it is also about learning: learning about life, the environment, materials around them and social relationships. This is just as true in the garden as it is anywhere else. The objective of this garden was to create a stimulating, inviting and practical playscape, making the best use of the space available, where young children feel free to have fun and play creatively.

As young children spend a great deal of time on the ground, a warm surface of decking has been used. The structure of the decking allows features for water play and sandpits to be hidden away when not in use, leaving valuable space clear. The garden is designed to stimulate the senses; textures, sounds and smells are all there to be discovered, explored and enjoyed. A canopy and playhouse divide the area into more intimate spaces. Striking art displayed in the garden is created by the children. Everything is designed with a young child's stature and needs in mind, and should provide hours of happy, productive play.

Above *Hidden under removable panels on a lower area of decking is a spacious sandpit. When the panels are in place, it leaves the area free for other games. Sand, which inevitably strays on to the decking, is easily swept back into the sandpit.*

Above *This charming playhouse creates a cosy enclosed space in the garden where young children feel at their ease. When not in use, it folds back against the wall, leaving space for other games.*

Right *All of the plants in this garden are irresistible. The fluffy grasses demand to be felt; the soft foliage of lavender has to be stroked and sniffed; shining bay leaves need to be crushed, releasing their aroma; the crinkled cabbage leaves have to be examined. These plants have been chosen to appeal to the senses. Even the large bamboo in the corner of the garden produces a reassuringly gentle rustle as it moves in the breeze.*

▶ see **Foldaway Playhouse**, page 28, **Bubbling Spring**, page 54

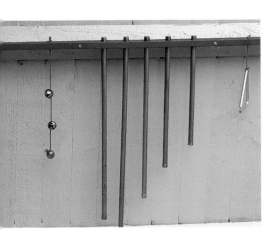

Far left *Playing with sound is not always welcome, especially within the confines of the house. Here, in the garden, experiments with sound are less jarring, using a percussion rack of bells, copper pipe chimes and a triangle.*

Above *The decorative diamond of play matting not only adds colour and texture to the garden, it also conceals a fascinating water feature. When required, it pumps irresistible shining jets of water through the matting, ideal for splashing fun and water play.*

Above *Set among swaying grasses and edged with zesty lemon thyme, this area is all about feeling, touching and exploring. A collection of natural shells, pebbles, fir cones, crystals and dried gourds are there to be played with, arranged, displayed, examined and sorted. The contents can be changed to provide new experiences.*

Left *Created from timber similar to that of the deck, a robust frame supports a swing. The uprights are held in place with ready-mix concrete.*

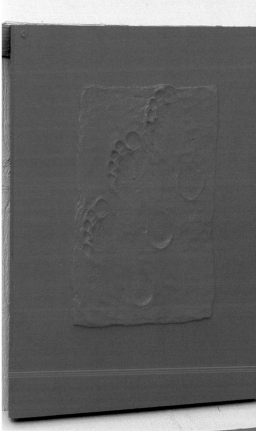

Above **This sturdy, unfussy bench-seat can be used as a chair or table. There are two such benches in the garden, arranged in a cosy corner canopied to provide shade.**

Above right **A straightforward blackboard becomes a decorative piece when livened up with a few spots of colour.**

Right **The garden is decorated with boldly coloured and textured pictures made by the children, making the garden very personal. This footprint picture is great fun, and is made using multipurpose filler smeared on to a piece of wood in a rectangle shape. Footprints are made in the filler when it is still wet, then it is allowed to dry and is later painted with bright pink acrylic paint.**

Above left *Ornamental cabbages planted in pink painted pots provide highlights of colour in the garden. The cabbages also offer interest for young children, with their fleshy, wrinkled texture and leathery feel.*

Left *Swaying grasses are soft to the touch and tough enough to withstand stroking.*

Above *A simple group of plants that appeal to the senses make an attractive display. The lavender has velvety leaves and a soft fragrance, while bay leaves have a brittle, shiny texture and release their aroma when crushed.*

the toddler's play deck **133**

the jungle outpost

This base for jungle explorers, complete with its own swamp, was designed for two boys aged nine and six. The playhouse had been the location of many happy toddler tea parties, but had since lost its charm. Now rejuvenated, it forms the central focus of an area, which though not large, is packed with features to inspire creative play.

Places to relax, socialize and exercise creative talents are also included, along with a tiny pond to attract wildlife and a swamp planted with fascinating carnivorous plants. Developing the area around the playhouse has given it a new appeal; a coat of wood stain, some blinds for privacy and a shady camouflage canopy are simple touches that complete its transformation.

A vast rope spider's web shields a secluded area left untouched, save for a flooring of play bark and a few logs – a place for hiding out and chatting or just digging in the soil.

Left *The secluded corner lined with reed screening is an ideal place to relax. The hammock is hung over an area of swamp, or more correctly bog. It was created by digging a hole, lining it with thick polythene and replacing the soil. Kept well watered, this provides perfect conditions for the large-leaved* Rheum palmatum, Carex pendula *and carnivorous plants. Decking stepping stones afford a safe passage through the swamp.*

Below left and centre *The swamp is also planted with* Sarracenia x mitchelliana, *with its striking red-veined trumpets, and* Dionaea muscipula *(Venus fly trap). Carnivorous plants need to be watered with copious amounts of rainwater. This is a task which children will normally take on joyfully.*

Below *Staring down the funnel of a sarracenia (pitcher plant) is disgusting, and therefore quite riveting. Buzzing trapped flies struggle in vain as they join the insect detritus gathered in the pitchers – a macabre novelty at which friends will marvel.*

Right *A piece of marine plyboard attached to the den with hinges and suspended by a colourful cord makes a simple table. Useful for playing games, eating or even homework.*

Below right *When the table is raised it becomes a useful chalkboard for drawing.*

Below *A column of marching leafcutter ants, stencilled around the walls of the den, adds a touch of humour.*

Left *This small, log-edged pond was created by simply sinking a plastic storage box into the ground. Though small, it is a haven for frogs and insect life and there is always something interesting to be seen. A fun, leopard-skin pot, planted with a large Phoenix canariensis palm, continues the jungle theme.*

Below *Part of the garden is shielded from adults by an intimidating spider's web and a rope ladder, and an area of dense shrubs. The secluded corner has been left untouched, save for a flooring of play bark and log stools, for the children to use as they please. The web itself is a great climbing challenge and a prop for fantasy games. Its robust and natural appearance makes it a superb addition to this jungle garden.*

▶ see **Rope Spider's Web**, page 14

Right, below and below right *Colour and humour are brought to the garden by these animal skin pots. The pots are deftly painted using acrylic paints and planted with ornamental grasses which complement their design. This type of pot is used throughout the garden to reinforce the jungle theme – zebra, giraffe and leopard skins are all reproduced.*

the child-sized potager

In a small space next to their playhouse, these children aged seven and five wanted a garden to grow fruit and vegetables. To make the most of the space and establish an attractive structure, four small colourful raised beds have been used, with a path of crunchy cockleshells. A central obelisk adds height and supports climbing crops. Once covered in plants, the obelisk even provides a tiny hideaway with four little seats, one attached to each raised bed.

Growing in raised beds helps to reduce the maintenance. However, the children do need assistance in caring for the garden, but they are able to carry out a surprising number of tasks with great proficiency and a lot of fun. The volume of crops this small space can produce is amazing. Gratifyingly, there is plenty for family meals and to give away to friends. Choosing a careful mixture of fruit, vegetables and flowers makes the tiny potager a handsome addition to the garden and ensures there is always something to be harvested. A careful use of colour gives the area of the potager and playhouse its own special identity.

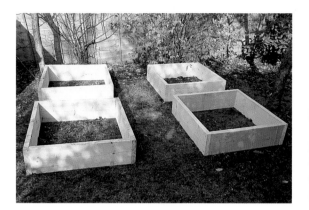

Above and above left
The raised beds of the potager are made from scaffold boards, screwed together to form four squares. The area was stripped of turf and the soil dug over to improve drainage. The boards are painted a purple colour to match the children's playhouse nearby. They are arranged in a simple grid pattern, which affords access to all sides of the beds.

Left *The beds are filled with a combination of topsoil and garden compost. To cut down on weeding, the paths are covered with a layer of weed-suppressing membrane which is topped off with a layer of crunchy cockleshells. The obelisk is formed from iron poles spray painted and fastened together at the top with wire. Each raised bed has a tiny wooden seat screwed to its corner.*

Below *A mulch of cockleshells adds fun and interest to the path of the potager. The shells produce a satisfying crackle when walked upon and should help deter slugs and snails.*

Above *It is important to keep young vegetable plants well watered. Undoubtedly this is one of the most popular tasks in a children's garden.*

Left *To provide some instant interest in the potager, some vegetables were brought as tiny plants and planted out into the beds. Others were grown from seed. The plants were arranged in patterns rather than traditional rows. Here spinach grows alongside beetroot.*

Left *The central obelisk plays host to a productive tangle of runner beans, mangetouts, peas and sweet peas. Inside the obelisk there is a shady space where tired young gardeners can take their ease, perched on the triangular seats provided on the corner of each raised bed. Here the garden is at its most voluptuous, lush with courgettes, parsley, salad leaves, rhubarb and spinach all thriving side by side.*

Below *The beetroot harvest. Unearthing root crops is always exciting as one can never be quite sure what lies beneath the crumbly soil.*

Right *The superbly tactile, purple-veined leaves of these thriving red cabbages will not only provide a delicious treat, but they also create a feast for the eyes. Their stunning foliage, as appealing as that of any ornamental plant, is set off beautifully by the purple of the raised beds.*

Above *In late summer, shining dwarf sunflowers are grown in a space once taken up by salad vegetables. Growing flowers among the crops is not only attractive, this companion planting ensures that plenty of helpful insects such as hoverflies are attracted into the garden to consume those which are less welcome, like greenfly. The humble marigold is an excellent companion plant.*

Above *Harvesting the fruits of your labour is a real treat. Crops can be picked as they are needed, but supply will hopefully outstrip demand. This perpetual spinach supplies leaves for salads and cooking in all seasons.*

Left *A trug full of fresh produce destined for the next family meal.*

the child-sized potager 145

the relaxing retreat

A once dilapidated summerhouse forms the focus of this garden retreat for older children. As children grow older, their needs change. There is still the need to provide for physical games like football and tennis, but more time is spent talking with friends and in quieter, less active pursuits. The garden offers a wonderful opportunity to provide a haven, a space to call their own and to share with friends. The ambience here is care-free, it is an escape, not childish but for children. The children are fortunate to have a large lawn for sporting pursuits, so this area has been designed to provide a place to relax. Within the garden there are spaces to eat, sit, laze and swing, and a separate more intimate area of deck. The summerhouse provides shelter and storage.

Evergreen grasses form the mainstay of the planting, which softens the structure of the garden. The colours chosen here are strong blues and yellows. The consistent use of these colours unites the different elements, giving the space an identity of its own and distinguishing it from the rest of the surrounding garden.

Above *A series of sturdy posts and kite fabric canopies provides a visual link between the summerhouse and the area outside, uniting the two. The four posts are simply held in position with ready-mix concrete, and form the supports for the large swinging benches either side. Using two colours of wood stain on each post creates an interesting visual effect.*

Right *Animated light and colour are projected around the garden by this hanging sheet of gleaming compact discs. Simply wired together and suspended by clothes pegs, compact discs make a novel and inexpensive decorative touch.*

Left *Slightly apart from the rest of the retreat, a yellow deck provides an intimate space. Overhung by a natural canopy, the deck is surrounded by a swathe of evergreen grasses and bright yellow flowers. Decking is a naturally warm and welcoming surface – just add a few cushions.*

Below left *Swinging is wonderfully relaxing. This 2m (6ft) swinging bench is big enough to share with friends. It is made from a large plank of timber suspended by rope from large hooks on the posts on either side. The rope passes through holes in the corners of the seat and is knotted beneath. The canopy overhead lends the space a feeling of intimacy and protection.*

Below *Ceramic glazed jars, planted with a shimmering* **Carex** *'Frosted Curls', stand sentinel on either side of the main canopy.*

Left *Inexpensive paving stones have been transformed using masonry paint. Not only are they now more decorative, but they can be used as gaming boards as well. Set well into the grass, they can simply be passed over when mowing. Here a chessboard, noughts and crosses, and tiddly winks or a marble game have been chosen, but the possibilities are endless.*

Right *Blue colour-washed pots planted with an undemanding sempervivum adorn the posts. Fine-grade slate mulch adds an interesting texture to the pots.*

Above *Beneath a gently rustling canopy, a gaily striped hammock is the perfect place for sitting or lounging. The shorter of the two post supports is spiralled by a coil of reclaimed concrete reinforcer, painted a darker shade of blue, which plays host to the climbing plant* Thunbergia alata *(black-eyed Susan).*

Right *No special preparation is required to make these game slabs. Just mark your design on to the paving stone with pencil and fill it in with the chosen colour of paint.*

safety

Minor bumps and bruises are an acceptable part of growing up – the products of testing capabilities and learning about the world, the trophies of childhood optimism and enthusiasm. The garden is the place where children get most opportunity to test their talents and explore. The sad fact is, however, that many children suffer major injury in their own gardens.

There is a careful balance to be achieved between the desire to provide a stimulating, challenging and entertaining environment, where the basic rules about keeping safe can be learnt and practised, and the need to remove all potential hazards. To complicate matters further, the point of balance is constantly shifting; what presents a danger to a two-year-old may be an irrelevance by the age of five, while safety measures employed beyond necessity may be very restricting for older children. Every reasonable step to remove danger should be taken.

The more confident a parent can be that a child has a safe place to play, the more freedom they can allow that child. A thorough and ongoing assessment of risk is advisable, with safety measures implemented and removed as appropriate.

Perhaps the biggest risk in the garden is that from the sun. Be sure to apply sun protection lotion when the children are playing outside for long periods, even in fairly overcast weather. Another form of sun protection is a shade canopy, which is simple to make and adds an eye-catching splash of colour to the garden.

Shade Canopy • Play Surfaces • Water • Plants • Other Hazards

shade canopy

This stylish, free-standing canopy can provide a large area of essential shade wherever it is needed. It can be used to protect sandpits, paddling pools and places to eat. When placed on a sunny lawn, children are naturally drawn to play in its shelter. When the canopy is complete, add a guy rope to each post, tying it around the screw of the finial and pegging it into the ground. Ensure that the pegs are flush with the ground and the guy ropes are easily visible.

materials

4 large terracotta pots
green masonry paint
4 wooden posts, 2.25m
   (7ft 6in) long
acrylic paints or wood stains
ready-mix concrete
2 large rectangles of closely
   woven fabric
cotton
4 brass hooks
4 brass curtain rings

1 Paint the pots with green masonry paint. Paint the wooden poles and finials with acrylic paints or colourful wood stain to match. Using two colours of paint or wood stain gives an interesting effect.

2 Set a post in each pot and secure it in place using ready-mix concrete. Ensure the posts are vertical using a spirit level, and leave sufficient space at the top of the pot to allow for planting.

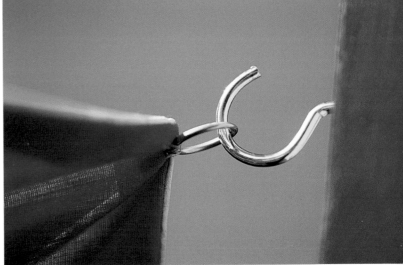

3 When the concrete is dry, add a finial to the top of each post. Sew the two pieces of fabric together, right sides in, leaving a 15cm (6in) gap in one of the seams. Turn the canopy right sides out and finish off the gap in the seam by hand.

4 Screw a brass hook 15cm (6in) from the top of each post. Sew a brass curtain ring to each end of the short sides of the canopy, 20cm (8in) in from the corners. Hook the canopy on to the posts and plant up the tops of the pots.

play surfaces

Choosing the right flooring under and around play equipment can make it safer. Surfaces which have some form of impact attenuation make injury from falls less likely. Simple grass or topsoil have some value. Other surfaces provide more protection, such as a deep layer of bark or wood chips, or specially designed rubber play matting systems, which can be laid over shock-absorbing pads. Play features should never be positioned on areas of concrete, tarmac, stone or other hard surfaces.

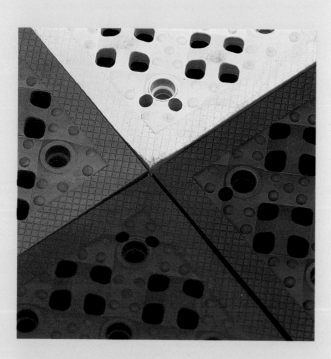

Above *This rubber play surface is bright, colourful, durable, non-slip and shock absorbent. It comes in square tiles in a range of different bright colours, and is flexible enough to be laid on sloping ground.*

Above *A beautifully designed iron grill guards the surface of this raised pond. Its ripple-like bars and lily pads actually enhance rather than detract from the pond's appearance.*

water

A young child will inevitably investigate any standing water around the garden. The alarming fact is that children can drown in just 5cm (2in) of water. Those aged between one and two years old are most at risk, with their newly acquired mobility but immature co-ordination. Some safety measures are simple; containers likely to collect a significant quantity of rain water should not be left in the garden. Take steps to secure water butts and always empty paddling pools. If there is a pond in the garden, then rigorous measures need to be taken. A rigid steel mesh can be secured over the entire surface of the pond, its integrity regularly checked. Chicken wire is just not good enough as it will sag under the weight of a child. Fencing the pond off is a solution often used. However, bear in mind that some fencing is easily climbed and gates need to be locked at all times and never inadvertently left open.

plants

It can seem that some plants are deliberately beguiling: the shining red berries of solanum (deadly nightshade) look as good as any sweet, the seedpods of laburnum could just as easily be miniature peas. In reality, however, both are extremely toxic. Other poisonous plants are not so appealing and, therefore, are less likely to present a hazard. Fortunately, instances of poisoning by plants are rare.

Plants also pose other risks: some produce an irritant or allergic reaction after contact with the plant or its sap (such as euphorbias), others present a physical danger such as sharp thorns, spines or pointed leaves.

Teach young children never to eat anything in the garden unless they have been told it is safe. Then, assess the likely risks in your garden, moving or removing plants. Exhaustive lists of poisonous and irritant plants are readily available, but space does not allow inclusion of such a list here.

Above and top **Ricinus communis** *(castor oil plant, top) is a strong irritant, while, once broken, the brittle stems of* **Euphorbia myrsinites** *pump out an irritant milky sap.*

other hazards

Above *The steep stairs of this terrace are safely guarded by these stylish gates.*

Children are tirelessly inquisitive – they want to experience and experiment with all they find around them. This means that a few basic safety rules need to be applied to the garden. Never leave tools or electrical equipment within reach. Lock all pesticides, fungicides and other chemicals securely away, or better still do not use them. Be aware of developmental changes in your children which give rise to new dangers, for example, as soon as a baby is mobile, steps need to be guarded. Look out for temporary hazards: the ends of the canes used for staking border plants could cause injury to running children. Using decorative cane tops makes this less likely. One final hazard is relevant when your child is outside – the sun. Provide sun creams, sun hats and, wherever possible, shade.

index

acknowledgments

Thanks to the following for the supply of materials:
Steel walkway – Goodman Steel (0118) 9561212
Glass, shell and coloured gravels – Specialist Aggregates (01785) 665554
Carnivorous plants – South West Carnivorous Plants (01884) 841549
Climbing holds – Enterprise (UK) Ltd (01282) 444800
Rubber play matting – Matta Products (01932) 788699
Rope – Footrope Knots (01473) 690090
Design of knotting for Rope Spider's Web – Des Pawson of Footrope Knots
Crocodile bench – Lusty Garden Furniture (01547) 560225
Pedro Bird Houses (p118) – Paul Hervey Decorative Products (01590) 645629
Wicker ewe and lamb sculptures (p118) at Nyewood House, Hampshire
Wooden fish sculptures (p119) at David and Marie Chase's Garden, Hampshire
Pond cover (p156) designed by Robin Templar-Williams
Decking garden (p157) designed by Sarah Layton

Author's acknowledgments
This book is the product of a very personal passion but it could not have been completed without the hard work, help and encouragement of others, to whom I owe a great debt of gratitude.

My thanks:

To my children, Harriet, Nancy and Joshua, the inspiration for this book, for their exuberance, honesty, patience and hard work throughout the project; I really could not have done it without them.

To the Hicks, Maitland and James families for allowing me to create the Real Children's Gardens in their gardens, giving me the freedom to create the unusual, for their unfailing enthusiasm, much appreciated practical help and great friendship, thank you.

To my parents, Ruth and Geoffrey Smee, for their support, encouragement, tireless practical assistance (from concrete mixing to cake baking) and their astounding and unfailing willingness to help in perpetuum.

To Clive Nichols for encouraging me to attempt this project, his enthusiasm, constant good humour and, of course, sensational photography.

To Joanna Smith for her faith in the project, her calm advice and great care over the design and editing of the book.

To Janet James for her patience and cheerfully rising to the challenge of tight deadlines in typing the manuscript.

To Steve Daley and Craig Hunt, whose generous favours saved the day.

To Hazel, Robert, Molly, Florence, Steven, Daniel, Connie, Ollie, Andy, Shana, Jasmine, William, George, Lucy, Jessica, Hannah and Anna-Nyun Forbang (pages 8, 64 and 159), who all appear in the book.

Finally to David, as always, for everything.

credits

Executive Editor Emily Van Eesteren
Executive Art Editor Tokiko Morishima
Production Controller Louise Hall
Editor and Designer Joanna Smith
All projects created and styled by Clare Matthews